THE THOUGHT OF THE DAY

Joshua Gautreau

authorHOUSE®

AuthorHouse™
1663 Liberty Drive
Bloomington, IN 47403
www.authorhouse.com
Phone: 1 (800) 839-8640

Published by AuthorHouse 10/28/2016

ISBN: 978-1-5246-4670-7 (sc)
ISBN: 978-1-5246-4669-1 (e)

Library of Congress Control Number: 2016918145

Print information available on the last page.

DAY 2

Your Personal Responsibility Is
To Become More Ethical Than
The Society You Grew Up In.

DAY 4

There's Nothing Selfish About
Making Yourself A Priority Once
In A While, It's Necessary.

DAY 5

Hang Around The Right People
Who Look At You Like Maybe
You Could Be Magic.

DAY 6

Remember That Before A Breakthrough Comes About, You Confront The Greatest Struggle.

DAY 7

Nothing In Your Life Should Make You Feel Regret, It Has Made You Who You Are.

DAY 10

Your Troubles And Tragedies
Are Only Here For A Moment,
So Is Everything Else.

DAY 11

Taking Your Time To Focus Attention
Of Concern To Love Another Is
The Greatest Gift You Can Give.

DAY 13

The Older That You Get You Realize
That You're Growing Into The
Person That You Were All Along.

DAY 15

There's No Need For Love To Be
Perfect, As Long As It's True.

DAY 16

Learn To Let Go Of Past Hurts, Yet Always Remember What They Taught.

DAY 17

All Acts Of Love And Kindness
Elevate Feelings Throughout
The Whole Universe.

DAY 18

Never Disregard Your Gut Intuition, If You Sense Something Is Not Right.

DAY 19

In Every Bad Time Pay
Attention To The Things That
It Brings Your Attention To.

DAY 21

Regardless Of What You Might
Think, Your Words Of The Ideas
You Have Can Change The World.

DAY 24

The Biggest Miscommunication
Is That We Listen To Reply
And Not To Understand.

DAY 26

Heart To Heart Conversations
Are Awesome, Vulnerability With
Honesty Equals Soul Connections.

DAY 28

Learn To Forgive For The Hurts
You Have Created And The
Hurts You Have Endured.

DAY 29

Always Show Gratitude For
Everything And Anything
In Your Life With Value.

DAY 30

Be Humble And Know That You Are Not Above Or Beneath Anyone Else.

DAY 32

Your Job Is Not To Judge Or
Figure Out Who Is Right Or Wrong,
But To Help Others Freely.

DAY 34

Sometimes We Have To Walk Through The Storm To Come Out Different Into The Sunshine.

DAY 36

A Perfect Relationship Is Two
Imperfect People Who Will Not
Give Up On Each Other.

DAY 38

Let Go Of Trying To Understand
Why Something Happened, Your
Peace Is More Important.

DAY 40

Your Imperfections Are Perfect For
The People Who Truly Love You.

DAY 41

For You To Tell Someone
That They're Appreciated
Is One Of The Best Things
That You Could Ever Do.

DAY 42

To Not Live In The Moment
Is To Look Forward To The
Unknown Or Back To The Past.

DAY 43

At Times In Life The Bad Things That Happen Put Us On The Path To The Best Things.

DAY 45

Do Not Judge Others For
Past Experiences Because
At One Time You've Done
Past Experiences As Well.

DAY 46

Everybody In This World Is Going
Through Something, Not Just You.

DAY 47

Tell People How You Feel Because
Opportunities Are Gone Fast
And Regrets Can Last Forever.

DAY 48

The Attacks In Your Life Get Greater
When Your Blessing's Get Closer.

DAY 50

People Who Succeed Are
The One's Who Can Fail And
Try Again Another Day.

DAY 52

If You Want To Know A Key
Secret To Getting Along
In Life, Let Things Go.

DAY 53

People Who Have A Positive Outlook On Life Produce Lives Of Peaceful Thoughts.

DAY 54

In Life The Things That Give
You A Challenge, Often
Change You For The Better.

DAY 55

The Best Way To Describe Love Is In What You Do, Not In What You Say.

DAY 56

Whenever You Let Go Of What
You Think You Are, You Might
Become Who You Truly Should Be.

DAY 58

At Times In Life It's Better
To Not Talk At All About
Anything To Anybody.

DAY 60

The People Who Come Into Our
Lives End Up Teaching Things
We Learn About Ourselves.

DAY 61

When We Work Hard For
Something Without Care It Is
Called Stress, Not Passion.

DAY 62

Never Accept A Person's
Kindness For Weakness,
Appreciate Their Well Being.

DAY 63

When You Pass Judgment
On Another You're Definding
Exactly Who You Are.

DAY 65

Have The Knowledge Through
Strength To Do Things With
The Power Of Will.

DAY 67

Sometimes You've Got To
Go Through The Impossible
To Reach The Possible.

DAY 70

In Order To Understand
Things In Life, You Have To Go
Through It On Your Own.

DAY 71

Laughing And Sleeping Are
Two Of The Best Healing
Things In The World.

DAY 72

You Are One More Day Closer To
The Goal You'd Like To Accomplish.

DAY 73

Be Careful How You View
Someone, Because That Idea Has
An Impact On Your Character.

DAY 74

Going Through Life Getting Told "NO" Gets You Closer To Your Yes.

DAY 76

Always Keep The Mind Frame That If Something Is Broken, Fix It And Never Throw It Away.

DAY 78

Never Wait To Let Somebody Know
How You Truly Feel About Them.

DAY 79

Always Keep Your Thoughts Positive Because Your Thoughts Lead To Where You're Destined.

DAY 81

The Lesson To Be Learned In
Being Upset Is Learned When
We're Not Upset Anymore.

DAY 84

The Moment You Feel Real Love Is When You Sit Beside Someone In Silence.

DAY 85

To Find Meaning In Life,
Renew The Mind To Find That
Love Is Why We're Here.

DAY 86

Know That There Is Something
Inside Of You That Can
Overcome Anything.

DAY 88

Regardless Of Your Current Situation, You Can Always Think To Create Something Different.

DAY 89

Changing Your Life For The Better Is Loving And Forgiving Somebody No Matter What.

DAY 92

Having A Beautiful Mind, Heart
And Soul Is Way More Attractive
Than Having A Fit Body.

DAY 94

Everyone Knows That There Is No Success Without The Struggle, Embrace It.

DAY 95

No Need To Ask Anybody To Give You Success, Go Out And Get It.

DAY 96

Never Stop Working Towards
Your Goals Just Because
Somebody Disapproves.

DAY 98

Always Keep In Mind That Since
You've Came This Far, There's
No Sense In Stopping Now.

DAY 100

Keep Your Focus On Being
Better Than Your Former
Self, Not Anybody Else.

DAY 101

Time Is Something That We Don't Have A Whole Lot Of, Use It Wisely.

DAY 102

Great Things Come To Those
Who Go Out And Earn What
They're Looking For.

DAY 104

Always Love Effortlessly, And
That Effortless Love, Will Always
Come Back Effortlessly.

DAY 105

Don't Allow Things Going On Around You To Pull You Down To It's Level.

DAY 106

Keep Friends Who Understand
You Truly, Your Sadness And
Happiness In The Same.

DAY 107

Things In Life Change In A Moment,
So Be Sure To Always Be Your Best.

DAY 108

Growth Comes In Life When
We Face Challenges, Nothing
Ever Comes Easy.

DAY 109

Sometimes We Face Difficult
Times Not Because We're Wrong,
But Because We're Right.

DAY 112

Everyone Has Faults, So Don't Put
Judgments On Another Unless
You're Looking In The Mirror.

DAY 114

Sometimes The People Who Annoy
You Often, Love You The Most.

DAY 115

Patience Is Key, Everything
Will Come Right On Time
Whenever It's Supposed To.

DAY 118

Don't Ever Push Away The People
Who Truly Love You Because They
May Not Be There One Day.

DAY 120

Always Remember That When
You're Doing The Right Thing,
Everything Right Will Fall Into Place.

DAY 121

You Are Not Your Thoughts, You Are Only The Thinker Of Your Thoughts.

DAY 122

Make Yourself Clear On What
You Say To People, It Is Vital
To Solid Communication.

DAY 123

The Greatest Thing We Can Do
For Someone Who Is In Pain
Is Just To Sit Beside Them.

DAY 125

Love Always Like That Person
Is The Last Number, Because
Numbers Never End.

DAY 126

When You Think About It,
Imperfection Is Perfect, If
You're Willing To Work At It.

DAY 127

If Someone Is Always On Your Mind, Send Out Good Thoughts Towards Their Way.

DAY 128

There Is Always A Choice Of Staying
In Negativity, Or Leaving It.

DAY 129

Never Worry About Other
People's Opinions Of You, Your
Opinion Is All That Matters.

DAY 130

At Times There Are No Words
For Your Thoughts, So Just Be.

DAY 132

We Are Not Who We Were
Yesterday, A Week Ago, A Month
Ago Or A Year Ago, We Are New.

DAY 133

You're Definitely Giving Yourself To
The Wrong Person If It's Your All
And It's Still Not Good Enough.

DAY 135

Life Is About Change, Allow The
Change To Take Place To Bring
Out The Best Person In You.

DAY 138

Two Broken People Can Help
To Repair Each Other Perfectly
Only Through Understanding.

DAY 140

The Person By Your Side In The
Best Times Should Be By Your
Side Through Your Worst.

DAY 141

At Times The Toughest Battle
We Have Is About What
Feel In What We Know.

DAY 143

Trust Always, No Matter What
Life Brings Your Way, You
Will Always Be Rewarded.

DAY 145

Until You Try To Love Someone,
You Never Really Truly Know
What They've Been Through.

DAY 146

Sometimes The Grass May Seem Greener On The Other Side Because It's Not Real.

DAY 148

Only When You've Failed And Start To Rebuild Yourself Is When You Truly Figure Out Who You Are.

DAY 150

Negativity Can Only Bother You
If You're On The Same Level.

DAY 152

You Don't Have To Prove To
Anybody You've Changed When
You See Things Differently.

DAY 153

Don't Worry About Living Up
To Anybody's Expectations,
Live Up To Your Own.

DAY 156

A Friend Is Someone Who
Listens To What You Have To
Say And Gives Truthful Advice.

DAY 157

Be Wise Enough To Know That
You're Different From All The Rest.

DAY 158

Even When Things Are Going
Wrong, Be Thankful For The
Things That Are Going Right.

DAY 160

When Music Is Playing And A
Song Describes Your Feelings
It's Always The Best.

DAY 161

Don't Bother With Being Worried
About Your Past, It Was Just A
Lesson To Make You Better.

DAY 163

When Somebody Closes
Themselves Off, Nobody Can
Hurt Them, Or Help Them.

DAY 166

If You're Stressed, Ask Your Self If
The Severity Is Worth The Strain.

DAY 168

If You Don't Take The Opportunity To Change Now, Then When Are You?

DAY 170

Be Wise Enough To Wait For
What's Yours And Strong
Enough To Let Go What Isn't.

DAY 172

You Have To Learn Who Is Just
Taking Advantage And Who
Is Worth Your Kindness.

DAY 173

Sometimes You've Just Got To Let Stuff Go, You've Been Through Things And More Is On The Way.

DAY 176

Always Keep In Mind When Working Towards Your Goals That When You're Seeing It, You're Being It.

DAY 178

Focus On The Spiritual Things
In Life That Money Can't Buy
And Be Richer Than Ever.

DAY 180

We Are All In No Position To
Judge Anyone For Anything
Because We All Are The Same.

DAY 181

When You Come In From Work Tired, Give Thanks That You Have A Job To Come In Tired From.

DAY 184

If You Fully Listen To Someone's
Reactions And Try To Understand
Them, Your Wisdom Grows.

DAY 186

People Who Want To Know When You've Made It Home Safe Are The Right Type Of People.

DAY 188

Healthy Relationships Are Those Who Agree To Make Each Other Better Versions Of Themselves.

DAY 189

Valentine's Day Should Feel
Like Everyday Whenever You're
In A Real Relationship.

DAY 192

When You Look Back On Your Life,
You See The Amount Of Things
That Made You Stronger Today.

DAY 194

There Are Not Losers In Life, Only
People Who Think So, Make Your
Own Victories How You See Fit.

DAY 196

The Idea Of Inner Peace Begins
When You Don't Allow Anyone Or
Anything To Control Your Emotions.

DAY 198

Always Give Thanks For The
Struggles In Your Life For They
Have Made You Your Best.

DAY 199

When You Smile, It Gives An
Example To The Whole World
That You Have Faith.

DAY 200

Anyone Who Shows Up In Your Life
Did Not Show Up By Coincidence.

DAY 201

Be Sure To Trust In How Things
Are Going, And The Results
Will Show For Themselves.

DAY 203

If You Want Security And The
Life You Want You've Got
To Go Get It Yourself.

DAY 205

Go To Places That Make You Realize
That Your Problems Aren't So Huge.

DAY 206

One Of The Best Ways To Cheer Yourself Up Is To Help Cheer Somebody Else Up.

DAY 208

Be Thankful Today For All Of
The Loving And Caring People
That Are In Your Life Today.

DAY 210

Know That Daily Everybody
Experiences Their Day Differently
Than Everybody Else.

DAY 211

Live For Today And Not The
Past, For The Past Will Destroy
Your Future If Allowed.

DAY 213

Love Is A Feeling That Ignites
A Human Being To Make
The Impossible Possible.

DAY 216

Think About If You Could Write
A Note To Your Younger Self,
What Would You Say?

DAY 218

Even Nothing In Nature Blooms All
Year, Be Patient With Yourself.

DAY 219

If You Decided To, You Could Just
Say To Yourself,
"Hey, I'm Going To Change."

DAY 220

Sometimes In Life You Just Need
To Let Go And See What Happens.

DAY 221

It Is Important In Life That We
Focus On The Repetitive Things
That Bring Us Prosperity.

DAY 224

It's Not About Everything You Have,
It's About What You're Happy With.

DAY 226

Search Out To Live A Life That Is Stress And Worry Free, Just Focus On Being Happy.

DAY 227

It's Okay To Fail At Times,
It's What We Learn From
And Keeps Us Humble.

DAY 228

If You Feel Like You Need To
Cry Then Do So, Sorrows
Keep Us Human.

DAY 230

There Is No Changing What
Already Happened, So
Move On And Let It Go.

DAY 231

It Takes A Matter Of Seconds To Hurt Someone, But Sometimes Years To Repair The Damage.

DAY 233

To Obtain Something You've Never Had, You've Got To Do Something You've Never Done.

DAY 236

Blessed Are The People Who
Help Teach Us To See The
World Through Different Eyes.

DAY 238

A Soul Has A Connection With
Another Soul Far Before Their
Bodies See One Another.

DAY 239

Reality Will Never Come
To The Mind Until It Has
Connected With The Heart.

DAY 240

There Is No Such Thing As Making
The Same Mistake Twice.

DAY 242

There Is No Stop To What You're Doing Because You're Always Doing Something.

DAY 243

Keep Your Positive Ideas Of What
You'd Like To Do To Yourself
And Bring Them Into Action.

DAY 246

You Appreciate The Blessing
Of Being Able To Be At Home
Resting The More You Age.

DAY 248

If You Feel Like You've Been
Doing The Right Thing, It'll
Be Wrong If You Stop.

DAY 250

The People In The World Who
Have Enough, But Then Again,
Not A Lot, Are The Most Happy.

DAY 252

Always Remember That
You Lose Out On All Of The
Chances You Never Took.

DAY 253

You've Got To Give It Your All And Sacrifice For What You Want In Life.

DAY 256

Listen With Close Attention To
What Your Heart Tells You, It
Always Knows The Right Answer.

DAY 257

If You're Constantly Thinking Of
Someone And Missing Them,
They Are Mighty Special.

DAY 259

No Matter What Life Has To Offer,
Always Trust Your Instincts.

DAY 260

To Discipline Your Mind Is
To Train Your Brain For The
Circumstances Of Life.

DAY 261

Life Has A Way Of Always
Testing Your Will, With You
Either Having All, Or Nothing.

DAY 262

The Right Person Always Gets Sent
Into Your Life At The Right Time.

DAY 264

Life Is All That You Can
Imagine That It Is, The Key
Is, You Have To Believe It.

DAY 265

Always Know That You've Got
More Than Enough, Now Go
Somewhere And Just Breath.

DAY 267

Always Surround Yourself With
People Who With Help You Be
Your Best Authentic Self.

DAY 269

Get Motivated To Always
Stay In A Good Habit That
Helps Mature Your Life.

DAY 270

There Comes A Time In Life When
You Walk Away From All The Drama.

DAY 272

The Most Difficult Roads Lead To
The Most Beautiful Destinations.

DAY 273

Worrying About Someting Is A
Complete Waste Of Time, It Leaves
You Without Joy Doing Nothing.

DAY 275

Life May Be Tough Throughout,
But Just Remember, So Are You.

DAY 276

Today Refuse To Worry And
Stress About Things You
Cannot Change Or Control.

DAY 277

A True Best Friend Is Someone
Who Loves You When You Have
Forgotten How To Love Yourself.

DAY 279

In Today's World We Rush
So Much That Sometimes
We Forget To Just Be.

DAY 280

To Have A Peace Of Mind Is Greater
Than All Of The Riches In The World.

DAY 282

If You Aren't Grateful With What
You Have, What Makes You Think
You'd Be Grateful With More?

DAY 283

Have Loyalty Within The Trust
You Have For Someone Proving It
Towards The Actions You Take.

DAY 285

If You Are Able To Let Go Of
What Is Weighing You Down, You
Can Soar With The Eagles.

DAY 288

The Day You Can Walk Into A
Room And Not Compare Yourself
To Anyone, You're Confident.

DAY 289

I Have No Intention Of Having
Competition With Anyone, I
Believe We're All Winners.

DAY 291

If You Have The Privilege To Make
Someone Happy, Then Do It, The
World Needs More Of That.

DAY 294

In One Lifetime You May Love Many Times, But Only One Love Will Stick With You Forever.

DAY 295

Laughter, Joy And Love Are Some Of The Quickest Ways Of Healing.

DAY 298

Everything That You Are Going Through Is Preparing You For What You've Asked For.

DAY 299

Miracles Begin To Take Place
As Soon As You Focus Your
Energy On Your Dreams As
Much As You Do Your Fear.

DAY 300

Try To Make Positive Decisions Today That Your Future Self Will Thank You For Tomorrow.

DAY 302

Sometimes You'll See A Persons
Mask Fall Off, But It Doesn't Mean
That Person Has Changed.

DAY 303

People Only Change For
Two Reasons, Either Their
Minds Are Renewed Or
Their Hearts Are Broken.

DAY 304

Whenever You Find Yourself Back
With The Wrong Crowd, It's Time
To Step Back And Reflect.

DAY 305

Keep Far Away From People Who Belittle You, They're Just Trying Make Themselves Feel Better.

DAY 308

Always Appreciate Your Rude
And Blunt Friends, They
Are Your Real Friends.

DAY 309

The Real People In The World
Could Care Less About Being
Liked, They Want Respect.

DAY 311

Fake Friends Believe In What They Hear, Real Friends Believe In You.

DAY 313

Things In Your Life That You Resist,
Continues To Persists Into Your Life.

DAY 314

Positive Thoughts And
Positive Feelings Attract
Positive Life Experiences.

DAY 315

Never Forget The People Who Were
There For You In Difficult Times.

DAY 317

You May Remember Someones
Physical Beauty For A Few
Days, But Recognize Someones
Beautiful Soul Forever.

DAY 318

Never Blame Anyone That Has
Came Into Your Life, You've Learned
Something From Each Of Them.

DAY 320

Help To Magnify People's
Strengths, Not Their Weaknesses.

DAY 322

Sometimes You've Just Got To Stop What You're Doing And Give Thanks To Being Alive.

DAY 323

Moving On Doesn't Mean You
Forget, It Means You Chose To
Be Happy Rather Than Hurt.

DAY 326

Our Thoughts Of Today Are Built Off Of Yesterday's Thoughts, So Watch What You Think From Now On.

DAY 327

Positive People Also Have Negative
Thoughts, They Just Choose
To Not Allow Those Negative
Thoughts To Control Them.

DAY 330

Before You End Up Saying Anything
To Anybody, Stop To Think How
That Would Sound To You.

DAY 331

Keep In Mind That You Are
The Average Of The People
You Choose To Be Around.

DAY 333

I Don't Know Which Hurts The
Most, Saying Something Wrong,
Or Saying Nothing At All.

DAY 336

If We Don't Stand Up For Ourselves Today, What Will Our Children's Future's Be Tomorrow?

DAY 337

Don't Ever Allow People Who
Are Afraid To Pursue Their
Dreams Try To Discourage
You From Pursuing Yours.

DAY 340

Let Cherished People Know That
If The Two Of You Depart, You'll
Always Keep Them In Your Heart.

DAY 342

Let Go Of The Fear That We're Not Good Enough, When We're In Fact, Over Qualified.

DAY 344

A Person's Imagination Is A Place Someone Can Go To Get All Of The Truth They're Searching For.

DAY 346

Life Doesn't Allow Us To Re-Write Our Wrongs, But It Does Allow For Us To Live Each Day Better Than The Last.

DAY 347

An Important Form Of Respect
Is Actually Listening To What
Other's Have To Say.

DAY 350

Our Story Doesn't End Whenever
We Fall Down, Our Story Begins
When We Stand Back Up.

DAY 351

Hold The Experience Of Life With Intelligence For When It Doesn't Go Your Way, Don't Blame Yourself.

DAY 353

Determination Will Help You To
Overcome Anything And Everything
That Is Happening To You.

DAY 355

Laughter Is Most Probably One Of The Most Important Things In A Person, It Cures All.

DAY 357

Every Human Being On Earth
Is The Center Of A Massive
Development Of Evolution.

DAY 359

You Don't Fall In Love
With A Person, You Walk
Into Love With Them.

DAY 360

A Huge Percentage Of Success,
Is Just Showing Up.

DAY 361

Never Stay Too Busy With Your Job That You Forget To Live Your Life.

DAY 362

When Things Are Bad, It
Won't Always Be That Way,
Live One Day At A Time.

DAY 363

When Things Are Good, It Won't
Always Be That Way, So Be Sure
To Live In Every Moment.

DAY 365

Always Stand Up For The Right
Thing, Even If You Stand Alone,
Change Starts In Your Thoughts.